# Far

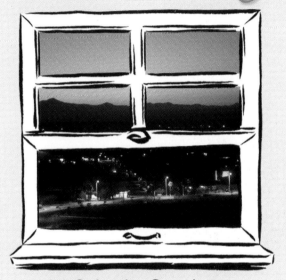

by Salvador Sarmiento

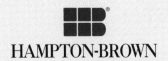

HAMPTON-BROWN

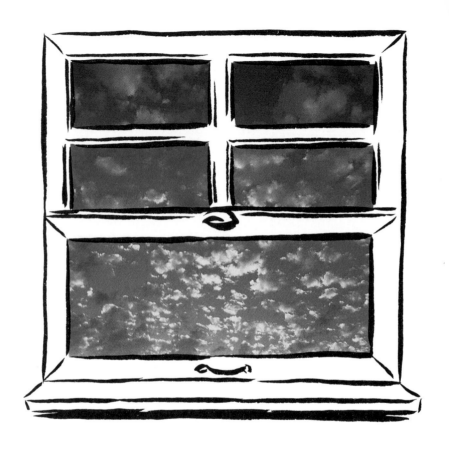

The clouds are
far away.

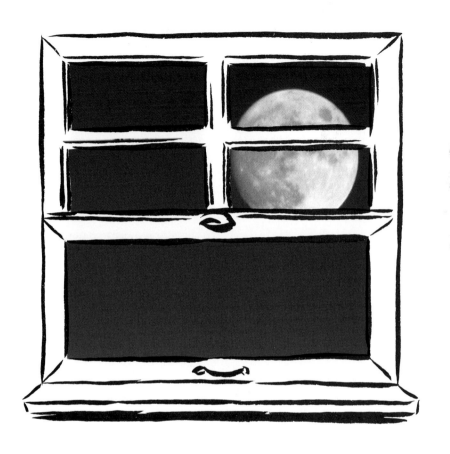

The moon is
far away.

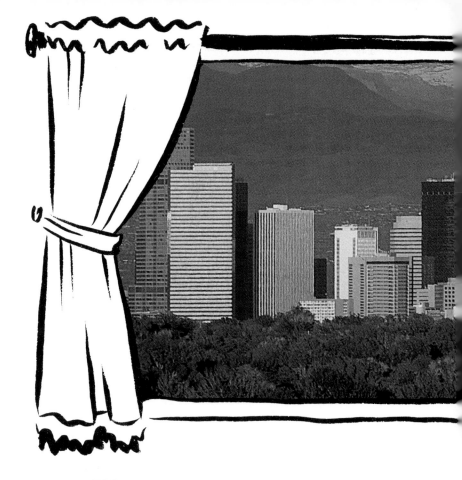

The buildings are
far away.

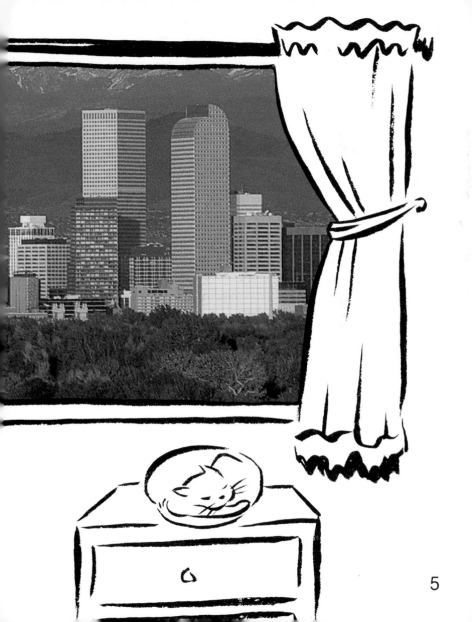

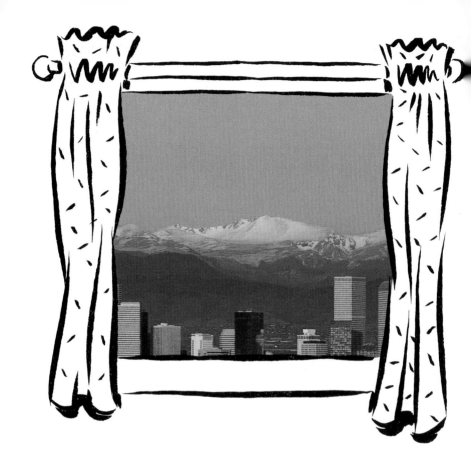

The mountains are
far away.

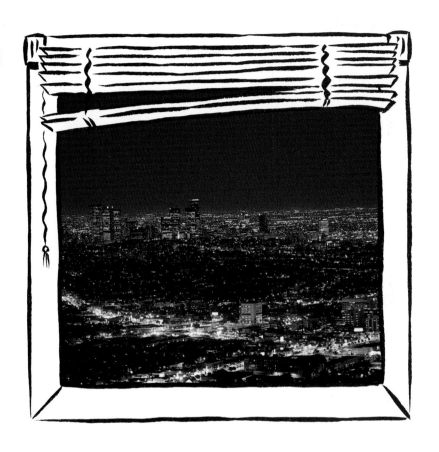

The city lights are
far away.

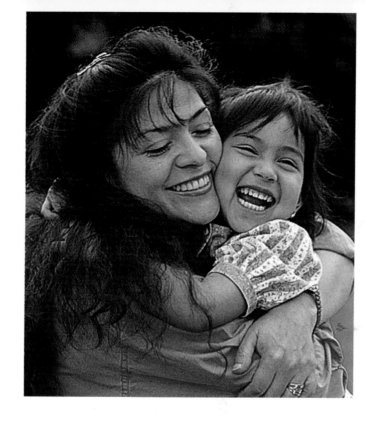

My mom is close to me!